**POINT OF IMPACT**

# The End of Apartheid
## A New South Africa

## RICHARD TAMES

**Heinemann Library**
**Chicago, Illinois**

Design and map artwork by Robert Sydenham
Illustrations by Robert Sydenham, Ambassador Design
Originated by Ambassador Litho Limited
Printed in Hong Kong

05 04 03 02 01
10 9 8 7 6 5 4 3 2 1

**Library of Congress Cataloging-in-Publication Data**
Tames, Richard.
     End of apartheid : a new South Africa / Richard Tames.
         p. cm. – (Point of impact)
     Includes bibliographical references and index.
     Summary: Examines the role of apartheid in the history of South History, key figures involved, and how this system eventually ended.
     ISBN 1-57572-412-X (library binding)
     1. South Africa—Politics and government—20th century—Juvenile literature. 2. Apartheid—Juvenile literature. 3. South Africa—Race relations—Juvenile literature. [1. South Africa—Politics and government. 2. Apartheid—South Africa. 3. South Africa—Race relations.] I. Title. II. Series.

DT1945.T365 2000
968.06'5—dc21
                                      00-024357

**Acknowledgments**
The Publishers would like to thank the following for permission to reproduce photographs:
Art Publishers, p. 8; Baileys African History Archives, p. 15; Bridgeman Art Library, p.7 (Stapleton Collection UK); Corbis, p. 27 (AFP), p. 19 (Hulton-Deutsch), p. 21 (Charles OíRear), p. 29 (Reuters Newmedia Inc), p. 17 (David Turnley), pp. 4, 11, 26 (Peter Turnley), p. 5 (Nik Wheeler); Hulton Getty, p. 6; Hutchison Library, p. 12 (Robert Aberman), p. 16 (Ingrid Hudson); Magnum Photos, p. 20; Rex Features, pp. 18, 23; p. 25 (Ian McIlgorm), pp. 14, 24, 28 (Sipa Press); Richard Tames, pp. 9, 22.

Cover photograph reproduced with permission of Link Picture Library.

Our thanks to Christopher Gibb for his help in the preparation of this book.

Some words are shown in bold, **like this.** You can find out what they mean by looking in the glossary.

# Contents

# A Scrap of Paper

Pushing a folded piece of paper into a big box is not particularly exciting—unless you have been waiting all your life for the right to do it. When the paper carries a mark next to the name of a politician or party to govern your country, it really matters. Until 1994, three out of four South Africans had never been allowed to vote in an election in their lives. Then, on April 27 of that year, millions of people lined up quietly to follow the example of a tall man with a warm smile, gray-haired but still strong and fit at the age of 76—Nelson Mandela.

The 1994 election made Nelson Mandela South Africa's first black president. A year later, he published the story of his life, calling it *Long Walk to Freedom*. It was an appropriate title. Mandela's long walk through life had taken him from barefoot cowherd to successful lawyer, from young amateur boxer to dedicated champion of human rights, from student runaway to holder of 50 honorary degrees and the Nobel Prize for Peace, from 27 years in prison to hero of his country and the world.

Nelson Mandela casts his vital vote on April 27, 1994.

## A vote for hope

Nelson Mandela chose to cast his vote in South Africa's first multiracial elections at Ohlange High School in Natal, because that was where John Dube was buried. In 1912, Dube had founded the organization to which Mandela had given so much of his life—the African National Congress. Before casting his vote, Mandela laid a wreath on Dube's grave. When he did finally cast his vote, 300 journalists were there to watch. Then he turned to them and said:

*"We are moving from an era of resistance, division,* **oppression,** *turmoil, and conflict and starting a new era of hope,* **reconciliation,** *and nation-building. I sincerely hope that the mere casting of a vote . . . will give hope to all South Africans."*

With the election of Mandela, the long oppression of South Africa's black majority, dating back to the beginning of the state of South Africa itself, was finally coming to an end.

The new nation has a new flag.

### THE UNITY FLAG
South Africa's new flag was adopted in 1994. The sideways "V"-into-"Y" shape represents groups in South Africa merging into one as they move forward together. It combines the six colors that had been used in the various flags adopted during the course of South Africa's history.

# Boer Against Bantu

## The first people

In 1488, the Portuguese first rounded the Cape of Good Hope, sailing for India. Later, ships landed at the Cape, trading for food with people who called themselves Khoikhoi and lived by hunting and herding. Further inland, the San, or bushmen, survived in very dry, desert country. Toward the east, in Natal, lived Bantu-speaking peoples, who were farmers as well as hunters and herdsmen.

## Dutch settlement

In 1652, the Dutch East India Company set up a base in southern Africa to provide water and food for ships on their way to the East Indies. Ninety men, serving under Jan van Riebeeck, battled droughts, floods, insects, diseases, and Khoikhoi cattle rustlers. Using slaves from other parts of Africa and the East Indies, they cleared land for crops.

By 1662, there were 250 white settlers, mostly Dutch, with some Germans. In 1685, interracial marriages between white settlers and local black slaves were banned. Soon afterwards, French **Huguenot** settlers joined the whites. When the British arrived later, European settlers who were already there became known as **Boers.** By 1707, there were 1,779 whites and 1,107 slaves.

This Boer family had black servants.

## Moving inland

Gradually, the Europeans took more and more Khoikhoi land, often by force, with guns. They also spread many European diseases, to which the Khoikhoi had no resistance. In 1713, smallpox wiped out many Khoikhoi, allowing the Europeans to move further inland.

By 1795, 15,000 whites and 17,000 slaves were scattered throughout the Cape colony, over an area roughly equal to the state of Colorado. Cape Town was the colony's only town and port. Around it was land taken over by Boers, who raised cattle and whose slaves produced wheat and wine. Beyond that, the Boer population extended 375 miles (600 kilometers) inland, where they lived by herding and farming. They killed the San and enslaved their children. In 1779–81, Boers fought their first frontier war against Bantu-speakers. The Bantu-speakers lived in large tribes and had iron weapons, which helped them to organize and fight.

This Zulu warrior is Utimuni, nephew of Shaka, the Zulu king.

### AN AFRICAN NAPOLEON

While European settlers were pushing inland from the southwest, Dingiswayo (died 1817), leader of the Bantu-speaking Zulu, founded a powerful kingdom in Natal. His successor, Shaka (1787–1828), organized an army of 40,000 Zulu into *impi* (regiments) of superbly trained warriors. Shaka's wars of conquest started a large wave of tribal migrations throughout southern Africa—called the *Mfecane* (crushing)—as weaker peoples fled his power. Although the Zulu empire was crushed by the British and the Boers, the memory of its strength remained to frighten many whites and inspire many native Africans.

# British and Boer

## Struggle over slavery

As a result of wars that started in Europe, Britain took over the Dutch Cape colony in 1806 and sent settlers soon after that. In 1833, Britain ended slavery throughout its empire, including the Cape. The **Boers** wanted to keep their independence, believing they had a God-given right to own African land and slaves. So they began a "Great **Trek**" inland, far from British rule.

In 1838, they killed 3,000 Zulus at Blood River, as they fought their way into Natal and avenged the murder of their leader, Retief, and his men. In 1843, Britain took over Natal, so many Boers moved even further inland. There they founded the Orange Free State and Transvaal as independent republics.

The monument at Pretoria commemorating the Great Trek includes a circle of stone wagons modeled after the ones the trekkers used.

## Struggles over riches

In 1867, diamonds were discovered in Boer territory. *Uitlanders* (foreigners), mostly British, flooded in. They soon outnumbered the Boers but, as foreigners, they had no vote. Some also hated the way the Boers treated African slaves. In 1877, the British tried to take over Transvaal, but they were resisted successfully. In 1886, gold was found in Transvaal, bringing in more unwanted fortune-hunters.

A second British–Boer conflict broke out in 1899. Boer forces were successful until the British built up a much larger army. The Boers then used hit-and-run **guerrilla** methods. The British responded by forcing Boer families off their farms and into camps, to keep them from giving Boer fighters food and information. The camps were poorly organized, and 26,000 Boer women and children died from disease and malnutrition. Although this was not intentional, it made many Boers feel bitter toward the British.

In 1902, the Boers finally agreed to accept British rule, while keeping the **Afrikaans** language for their schools and courts, and receiving cash for damage to their farms. In 1910, Britain tried to reconcile the defeated Boers by joining the Cape, Natal, Orange Free State, and Transvaal into one Union of South Africa—with the Boers effectively in control.

This statue of South African leader Jan Smuts stands in Parliament Square in London.

### ENEMY INTO FRIEND

Jan Smuts (1870–1950) was a Boer who had been educated in Britain. Although he was a brilliant commander against the British, he still believed that the Boers' best future lay in working together with them. Smuts led South African forces for Britain in both world wars, serving in the British war cabinet both times, and was South Africa's prime minister in 1919–24 and 1939–48. He also helped found the **United Nations.**

# Whose Country?

## One country, many peoples

Despite being united under one government in 1910, South Africans remained deeply divided. Whites made up only 21.5 percent of the population, and of these, an English-speaking minority dominated government and business in the cities. Most whites were **Afrikaans**-speaking **Boers**—most were farmers, and many were still bitter about the war. The majority black population (67 percent) included many different groups of people. Some of these were large, such as the Zulu or Xhosa of the Transkei region. Other groups were much smaller.

Whatever their tribe or language, black Africans had already lost the best lands to white farmers and businesses who used money, the law, or brute force to take them. By 1910, black Africans owned less than ten percent of a country that their ancestors had completely controlled. In 1913, the South African Parliament passed a Native Land Act that limited the blacks' ownership of land even more. There were also "**coloreds**" (9 percent), born of mixed marriages between blacks and whites, and Indian immigrants (2.5 percent). Indians and coloreds had varying rights in the Cape, but were not treated as equals by most whites.

This was the Union of South Africa in 1910. Neighboring countries are named as in 1910, with their present names in brackets.

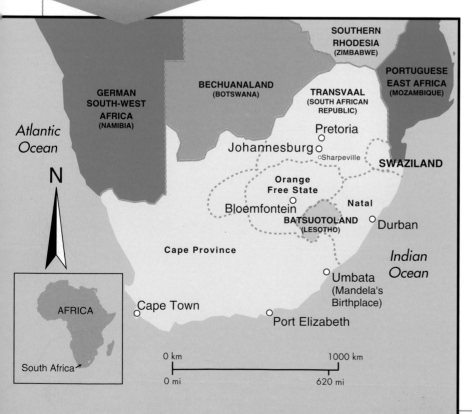

## Getting organized

In 1912, the South African Native National Congress was founded to unite black Africans and defend their interests. Its anthem, *Nkosi Sikelel'i Afrika* (God Bless Africa), is now South Africa's national anthem. In 1923, this organization became the African National Congress (ANC).

In 1913, James Hertzog (1866–1942), a former Boer general, formed the Nationalist Party to defend **Afrikaner** interests. He wanted South Africa to be completely independent from Britain.

## War

When World War I broke out, Hertzog wanted South Africa to stay out of it. However, some Boers revolted against British rule. Prime Minister Louis Botha (1862–1919), the former top Boer commander, stopped the revolt and also conquered the neighboring German colony of South-West Africa. Like Smuts, he favored **reconciliation** between Boers and the British. The war also boosted South African industry and mining.

The flag of the African National Congress includes three colors that represent ideas: black for the people, green for the land, and gold for resources.

## NEW WAYS TO FIGHT

Indians came to South Africa as laborers. Some prospered, becoming traders, but most were treated as second-class citizens by whites. Indian lawyer Mohandas Gandhi (1869–1948) founded the Natal Indian Congress to defend their rights. Here, he began to develop the nonviolent methods of political struggle, such as strikes, sit-ins, and **boycotts,** that he later used to free India itself from British rule. Indians called him *Mahatma* (Great Soul). Gandhi's ideas were later followed by Dr. Martin Luther King Jr. in the United States, and by Nelson Mandela in South Africa.

# The Roots of Apartheid

## Migrant labor

The wartime boom encouraged black African men to leave their families on the poor lands, in "native reserve" areas set aside for them, and go to find work in mines and cities. They came back home periodically, bringing money they had earned. Industry needed many African **migrants** for permanent work, but Africans were regarded as only temporary residents outside the reserves. They were forced to carry passes so that police could control their movements. The police would check to see if a person had a job—and therefore the right to be outside a reserve.

### THE BROTHERHOOD

In 1918, some **Afrikaners** formed the *Broederbond* (Brotherhood) as a secret society to fight for the interests of Afrikaners as a separate nation. Members of the *Broederbond* came to hold important positions in politics, the army, the police, and business, and used their power to help each other.

When the men were away, the women and children had to work the land alone.

## War ends—troubles begin

The wartime boom was followed by hard times. In 1920, African mineworkers went on strike, and African demonstrators were killed by police in Port Elizabeth. In these troubled times, a South African **Communist** party was founded in 1921. It accepted all races—something unique at that time

In 1922, white miners went on strike to protect their right to have all the skilled jobs. Black Africans protested against the laws that made them carry passes.

## New government—new laws

The Labour Party, supported by white miners, joined forces with the Nationalist Party and, in 1924, defeated the South African Party, which had ruled since 1910. The new Nationalist government, led by James Hertzog, made South Africa more independent of British control and favored the interests of whites—and especially Afrikaners—at the expense of

The new 1927 flag of the Union of South Africa combined the British Union Flag with the flags of the Orange Free State and Transvaal, symbolizing respect for both British and Boer traditions.

blacks. South Africa dropped the Union Flag in favor of its own national flag, and sent its own ambassadors to foreign countries. **Afrikaans** was confirmed as an official language along with English. The color bar in the workplace, which reserved skilled jobs for whites, was strengthened.

A government-owned steelworks was built at Pretoria, increasing the importance of heavy industry and mining and providing more jobs for whites. An Immorality Act limited mixed marriages among races. In 1929, Afrikaners began to use a new word to describe this policy of racial separation—**apartheid**, meaning "separateness."

# The Adviser's Son

### Herdboy

Nelson Mandela was born on July 18, 1918 in his family's **kraal** at Mvezo, a village near Umtata, capital of the Transkei region. He was the son of the senior adviser of the paramount chief of his Thembu tribe, but as a boy, he still helped with herding cattle—these were his people's main form of wealth. Nelson also had the tribal name Rolihlahla, which in the Xhosa language means "stirring up trouble."

### Runaway

Mandela went to schools run by white missionaries, and then to Fort Hare University College, where he met Oliver Tambo and became involved in student politics. He was suspended for his part in a protest about the school's food. The tribal chief ordered him to stop the protest, continue studying, and marry a bride chosen for him. Instead, Mandela ran away to the city of Johannesburg and worked as a guard at a mine.

Nelson Mandela enjoyed amateur boxing as a young man and kept fit during his long years in prison.

## Lawyer

In Johannesburg, Mandela met Walter Sisulu, also from Transkei, who encouraged him to study and got him a job in a law office. Mandela studied law at the University of Witwatersrand while he worked. He also joined Sisulu as a member of the African National Congress (ANC) and married Walter's cousin, Evelyn, a nurse.

## Activist

Younger members of the ANC, like Sisulu, Tambo, and Mandela, thought the group was getting nowhere after 30 years of polite, peaceful protests. Some black Africans could vote in the Cape colony, and ANC leaders had hoped that black Africans in the rest of South Africa would also be included. Instead, in 1936, Hertzog's government limited black voting rights in the Cape to the choosing of three white **representatives.** As a result, in 1944, younger ANC members founded the ANC Youth League, intending to use more **militant** methods. In 1947, Mandela was elected secretary of the Youth League.

Mandela shared this law office with Oliver Tambo. It was the first black law firm in Johannesburg.

### OLIVER TAMBO

Mandela's closest **comrades** in the ANC were also his lifelong friends. In 1952, Oliver Tambo (1917–93) joined Mandela to set up Johannesburg's first black law firm. Tambo later spent 30 years abroad representing the ANC, much of this while Mandela was in prison.

# Apartheid Enacted

## A turning point

World War II again boosted industry in South Africa, attracting even more black Africans to cities. Many whites feared that they could lose their jobs to Africans who earned much lower wages.

In 1948, they elected a Nationalist Party government under Dr. Daniel Malan (1874–1959). He promised that the existing separation of black and white South Africans would become a total system of **apartheid.** This would officially classify people as whites, **coloreds**, Indians, and Bantu (blacks). Each race would live in its own areas, be educated separately, use separate transportation, hospitals, libraries, and cinemas, and be forbidden to intermarry.

A Suppression of Communism Act, passed in 1950, gave government the power to imprison anyone accused of trying to make changes through "disturbance or disorder." In this way, whites' privileges at work and power in government would be protected forever.

Blacks in South African townships suffered in separate and unequal living conditions.

## Resistance

Resistance to apartheid, including marches, strikes, and **boycotts,** was weak because its opponents could not agree on how to proceed. Some ANC members favored cooperating with other groups, such as **Communists** and organizations of Indians, coloreds, or the white minority that also opposed apartheid. Others wanted a "black Africans only" approach.

CITY OF PORT ELIZABETH
NOTICE
FOR WHITE PERSONS ONLY.
BY ORDER.
STAD PORT ELIZABETH
KENNISGEWING
SLEGS VIR BLANKES.
OP LAS.
IDOLOPHU YASEBHAYI
ISAZISO
ABANTU ABA - MHLOPE
BODWA.
NGOMYALELO.

Separation of blacks and whites was enforced in public places, such as beaches, where they might otherwise have mixed as friends.

## Defiance

In 1950, Mandela was elected national president of the Youth League. With Sisulu, he carefully planned a "Defiance Campaign" of marches and meetings for April 6, 1952—just as **Afrikaners** celebrated the 300th anniversary of Dutch settlement. Indians and some whites supported the campaign. The Nationalist government cracked down with arrests and made apartheid laws even harsher, but the campaign spread awareness of apartheid abroad, and the system was condemned by the **United Nations.** The campaign also boosted ANC membership from 7,000 to over 100,000. Mandela was arrested under the Suppression of Communism Act, but he was not imprisoned because he had stressed the need to avoid any violence.

## ARCHITECT OF APARTHEID

Dutch-born Hendrik Verwoerd (1901–66) was a sociology professor and editor of the Afrikaner daily newspaper *Die Transvaler.* He resigned from his university post in protest when South Africa admitted Jewish refugees from the Nazis. As minister of native affairs (1950–58), Verwoerd drew up the detailed apartheid laws. Verwoerd became prime minister in 1958 and was **assassinated** in parliament in 1966 by a mixed-race messenger.

# Confrontations

## Banned!

Resistance to **apartheid** continued throughout the 1950s. The Nationalist government made strikes by Africans illegal and used "banning orders" to stifle over 1,500 opponents. A person who was banned was forbidden to go to any meeting—defined as three or more people—or enter a court, college, or newspaper office. Banned people could not be quoted or even contact each other. Banning orders, lasting from two to five years, could be renewed repeatedly.

In 1952, the ANC elected Chief Albert Luthuli as president-general, with Mandela as his deputy. But Mandela was soon forced to resign when he became a banned person. In 1955, the ANC adopted a Freedom Charter calling for a nonracial South Africa, with equal rights for all.

Nelson Mandela stands in the middle of the third row from the front at the 1956 treason trial.

## Trials and troubles

In 1956, Mandela, Tambo, Sisulu, and over 150 others—105 Africans, 23 whites, 21 Indians, and 7 **coloreds**—were put on trial for alleged treason. The trial dragged on for four years. Since defendants were free when they were not actually needed in court, Mandela continued working as a lawyer. After divorcing Evelyn, he married Winnie Nomzamo Madikizela, a friend of Tambo, in 1958.

In 1959, Chief Luthuli called for a foreign **boycott** of South African goods to put pressure on the Nationalist government. In the same year, some ANC members who were opposed to cooperating with Indians and **Communists** broke away to form the Pan Africanist Congress (PAC).

This was the scene after the shooting at Sharpeville.

## Massacre

In 1960, the PAC organized a protest against the pass laws at Sharpeville (40 miles/65 kilometers south of Johannesburg, near Vereeniging). Some 5,000 unarmed protesters gathered outside a police station. Stone-throwing led to shooting. At the end of the day, 69 Africans were dead and 178 wounded. The ANC called for a national day of mourning. The government declared a state of emergency, banned both the ANC and PAC, and imprisoned Mandela along with 2,000 other anti-apartheid **activists.** Oliver Tambo fled abroad to set up ANC offices wherever it was safe.

Mandela used his treason trial to explain, "We are not anti-white, we are against white supremacy." In March 1961, he was found not guilty of treason. Later that year, South Africa became a republic and left the **Commonwealth** rather than abandon apartheid. The ANC responded by forming a military group—*Umkhonto we Sizwe,* or Spear of the Nation—to launch a **sabotage** campaign.

# Struggling On

## False independence

In 1959, a Bantu Self-Government Act planned **bantustans** under African chief ministers. Between 1976 and 1981, four of these "homelands"—Transkei, Bophuthatswana, Venda, and Ciskei—were recognized by South Africa as "independent" states. In reality, they were too poor to support themselves. They relied on South Africa and money from their so-called citizens, who went to work in South Africa, leaving their families living in squalor. The bantustans were situated in some of South Africa's harshest areas. No other countries recognized their independence.

Pass books were needed to enforce apartheid. Destroying one was an act of defiance—and a crime. Unlike sabotage, this form of resistance needed no training or equipment.

## Pressures outside and in

In 1962, South Africa made **sabotage** a **capital offense.** Starting in 1967, accusations of **terrorism** could mean prison without trial. Then, after a 1974 revolution in faraway Portugal, Mozambique and Angola—its former colonies—gained independence. Nearby Zimbabwe became independent in 1980.

These "front-line states" had previously supported South Africa. Now, ruled by black majorities, they provided bases from which **guerrillas** of *Umkhonto we Sizwe* attacked economic targets, such as power stations. South Africa sent troops to raid the front-line states, and eventually became involved in fighting in Namibia as well. South African military spending rose almost tenfold.

Many countries answered Luthuli's call, **boycotting** South African goods. South African teams were banned from the 1964 Olympics and international cricket and rugby matches. In 1974, South Africa was banned from the **United Nations (UN) General Assembly.**

## The prisoner

When the ANC was banned in 1960, Mandela went on the run, visiting Ethiopia and Britain to rally support, then Algeria for military training. He was arrested in 1962, after secretly returning to South Africa, and was imprisoned for five years for organizing strikes.

This is Robben Island Prison, as viewed from above. Mandela was held in this grim place from 1964 to 1982.

In 1963, South African police arrested Sisulu and others at a secret *Umkhonto* base at Rivonia, near Johannesburg. Mandela was linked to their sabotage campaign, and in 1964, he was sentenced to life imprisonment. As prisoner 466/64, he was sent to do hard labor on Robben Island and allowed only one letter and one visit every six months. In 1973, Mandela was offered a shorter sentence if he would support the bantustan program. He refused.

## SOWETO—MASSACRE OF SCHOOLCHILDREN

Soweto (the name was formed from SOuth-WEst TOwnships) is the southern, black area of Johannesburg. In June 1976, black schoolchildren there protested against being taught in **Afrikaans,** not English, because Afrikaans was regarded as the language of pass laws, permits, and police. Police shooting and further riots killed over 500. Thousands fled to join *Umkhonto,* the military wing of the ANC. Plans for compulsory schooling in Afrikaans were dropped in the aftermath of Soweto, and the UN banned sales of weapons to South Africa in 1977.

# South Africa Under Siege

## Prison progress

In 1980, the **United Nations** called on South Africa to release Mandela and start "meaningful discussion of the future of the country." There were no discussions, but Robben Island prisoners were allowed to have newspapers and to buy groceries and toiletries with money they earned gardening. Mandela and other "special section" prisoners no longer had to collect seaweed or break rocks to mend roads. In 1982, Mandela, Sisulu, and three more Rivonia men were switched to Pollsmoor Maximum Security Prison in Cape Town, where they had radio and better food but were even more closely guarded. However, Mandela was now the world's most famous prisoner and, between 1979 and 1986, he received awards from India, Austria, Venezuela, East Germany, Britain, the United States, Cuba, Spain, Sweden, and Malaysia.

This statue honoring the famous prisoner was unveiled in London in 1984, the twentieth year of Mandela's imprisonment.

"THE STRUGGLE IS MY LIFE"
NELSON MANDELA
GAOLED 5th AUGUST 1962
SENTENCED TO LIFE IMPRISONMENT
12th JUNE 1964 FOR HIS ACTIONS
AGAINST APARTHEID
ERECTED BY THE GREATER LONDON COUNCIL
UNVEILED BY OLIVER TAMBO
PRESIDENT OF THE AFRICAN NATIONAL CONGRESS
28th OCTOBER 1985

## Divide and conquer?

**Boycotts** and **sabotage** continued. In 1983, the United Democratic Front was formed by 600 anti-**apartheid** organizations to support the Freedom Charter. To split this opposition, the government gave **coloreds** and Asians limited political rights. However, nearly all of them rejected their new rights, instead demanding rights for everyone, regardless of race. In 1985, the ban on mixed marriages was ended. By then, military spending had risen to the huge figure of 4.8 million Rand, and the army had almost doubled again to 639,000. The resulting heavy taxes and strong military presence made many foreign businesses nervous about **investing**.

## State of emergency

Concessions to **coloreds** and Asians only made black South Africans even more determined to struggle for their rights. The government offered Mandela early release if he would condemn ANC **militant** tactics. He refused. Rioting and school boycotts led to a state of emergency being declared from July 1985 to March 1986. There were 8,000 arrests and 750 deaths. Overseas, the United States and France led trade and investment **sanctions** on South Africa. These cost it between 32 and 42 billion U.S. dollars between 1985 and 1989.

Archbishop Desmond Tutu won the Nobel Peace Prize for his work against apartheid.

### DESMOND TUTU (1931–)

Desmond Tutu, the son of a Transvaal teacher, also taught in schools before becoming an Anglican priest. He rose rapidly to become the first black Anglican bishop of Johannesburg (1985–86). Although he opposed violence, he repeatedly risked imprisonment by calling for strong sanctions against South Africa. In 1984, Tutu won the Nobel Peace Prize, which is awarded annually to the person or organization that has done the most for human rights. In 1986, he became archbishop of Cape Town. In 1995, after apartheid had been overcome, he became chairman of the Truth and **Reconciliation** Commission, which uncovered political and police crimes that had been committed under apartheid.

# A New Beginning

## Reassurance

In May 1988, the **UN** called again for Mandela's release without conditions. Mandela himself wrote to South African President P.W. Botha, suggesting that "the meeting between the government and ANC will be the first major step towards peace in the country." Mandela insisted that South Africa should remain one country where everyone had equal rights, rather than be divided into **bantustans** and areas for other races. He also insisted that "majority rule will not mean domination of the white minority by blacks."

Possibly the biggest birthday party in the world was held at Wembley, London, in 1988—and Mandela, the guest of honor, was in prison, so he couldn't attend.

## THE BIGGEST BIRTHDAY

In 1988, Mandela's 70th birthday was celebrated with a huge concert in London's Wembley Stadium. It was attended by 75,000 people and watched on television by a billion more in 64 countries. Eleven mailbags of birthday cards were delivered to his wife, Winnie, at Mandela's Soweto home.

## Momentous meetings

In July 1989, President Botha at last met Mandela briefly. Both men pledged "support for peaceful developments."

Botha had recently suffered a stroke and resigned in August on grounds of ill health. This opened the way for a new approach by a new leader. In September, Botha was succeeded as president by F.W. de Klerk. The new president was determined to break out of what he recognized as an endless "cycle of violence," in which riots provoked crackdowns, which provoked more riots. A month later, on de Klerk's orders, Walter Sisulu and seven other political prisoners were released—to a rousing welcome.

Mandela met with President F.W. de Klerk.

De Klerk and Mandela at last met face to face in December. Mandela declared de Klerk to be "the most honest and serious white leader" he had ever met. On February 2, 1990, de Klerk announced the end of the bans on the ANC, the PAC, the **Communist** party, and over 30 other anti-**apartheid** organizations.

## Free at last!

On February 11, 1990, after 27 years in prison, Nelson Mandela walked out, a free man. That same day he declared, "Today the majority of South Africans, black and white, recognize that apartheid has no future." Chris Hani, deputy commander of *Umkhonto we Sizwe*, observed, "I think we're going to learn from him that we need to be better South Africans—to forgive and forget and to look forward. . . ."

# The Ending of Apartheid

### Reforms

The state of emergency, which had been renewed every year since 1986, ended in 1990. In 1991, laws enforcing **apartheid** were abolished. In Johannesburg, **representatives** of political, church, and business groups met as the Convention for a Democratic South Africa (CODESA) and discussed a new democratic **constitution.** A majority of white voters now supported de Klerk's moves away from the past and towards a new future. But not everybody did.

### Conflicts . . .

Not surprisingly, white **Afrikaner** extremists opposed the ending of apartheid. So did many members of the security forces, who feared past illegal actions might be punished. The PAC resented the dominant role of the ANC. The strongest opposition, however, came from the Inkatha Freedom Party (IFP) led by Chief Buthelezi, whose followers clashed violently with ANC supporters.

Nelson Mandela took the oath of office as president of South Africa on May 10, 1994.

Strikes, demonstrations, and two mass killings led to a temporary breakdown of CODESA. The talks—this time including PAC representatives—finally resumed in April 1993, only to be interrupted by the **assassination** of ANC leader Chris Hani. In June, the Inkatha Freedom Party walked out of the talks.

## . . . and compromise

CODESA plans for moving by stages to a multiracial system were rejected by a Freedom Alliance (FA) of Inkatha, the governments of Ciskei and Bophuthatswana, and the **Afrikaner** *Volksfront* of hard-line Afrikaner groups. Intense discussions and **compromises** finally persuaded the FA to take part in the April 1994 general elections. These resulted in a clear victory for the ANC and the inauguration of Nelson Mandela as president of South Africa.

### CHIEF MANGOSUTHU BUTHELEZI (1928–)

Buthelezi, a descendant of the Zulu royal house, became a chief at age 25. He opposed apartheid, but in 1972 he became chief minister of the KwaZulu **bantustan** for fear of something worse being imposed. He also founded the Inkatha Freedom Party to organize support among Zulu tribesmen. Buthelezi's reluctant acceptance of bantustan office was bitterly opposed by ANC leaders. When apartheid ended, Buthelezi wanted special rights for KwaZulu within any new political structure. In the 1994 election, Inkatha won control of the new province of KwaZulu/Natal, and Buthelezi accepted the post of home affairs minister in a government led by the ANC.

Chief Buthelezi addressed Inkatha supporters at a Soweto rally during the 1999 election campaign.

# No Easy Walk to Freedom

## President, superstar

In 1993, Mandela was awarded the Nobel Peace Prize jointly with President de Klerk. Ever since his release, people all over the world have been deeply impressed by Mandela's immense dignity and charm, as well as by his willingness to forgive those who had taken away 27 years of his life and liberty by keeping him in prison. Mandela believed that no new South Africa could be created without a spirit of **reconciliation** between former enemies, and he set the example himself.

The year 1994 was to prove a great one for the new South Africa. It rejoined the **Commonwealth** and joined the **Organization of African Unity.** International sporting links were renewed—a major step for a sports-crazy nation that had been shut out of world competition for 30 years. South African athletes made a strong comeback. In 1995, South Africa hosted and won the Rugby World Cup.

Nelson Mandela celebrated with the South African soccer team after they won the Africa Cup in 1996.

# Facing the future

Nelson Mandela often quoted the Indian independence leader Nehru, who warned followers that there would be "no easy walk to freedom." The new South Africa still faces huge problems. Despite its immense riches in minerals, gold, diamonds, and fertile soil, and despite being the biggest industrial power in Africa, the country is still blighted with poverty.

President Thabo Mbeki continues Mandela's work.

Unemployment stood at 30 percent in 1998. Millions still live without electricity or running water. One in five people cannot read or write. The ending of **apartheid** raised high hopes, but these could not be quickly satisfied. Years of violent political struggles have left a continuing problem of violent street crime. This in turn has made foreign businesses nervous about **investing** money to create the new jobs that South Africa so badly needs.

But there have also been major successes. With the ending of rule by armed force, the size of the military has been cut in half. Former freedom fighters from *Umkhonto we Sizwe* have been absorbed into a reformed army and police force. Most important of all is the fact that in 1999, when Nelson Mandela stepped down as president, Thabo Mbeki, his former deputy president and old prison **comrade** from Robben Island, succeeded to the presidency smoothly and without any threat of political violence. Mandela's last gift to his country has been to bring it to the point where it could learn to go on peacefully without him.

# Important Dates

| | |
|---|---|
| 1652 | Jan van Riebeeck establishes Dutch East India Company settlement at the Cape |
| 1806 | British take over the Cape colony |
| 1828 | Death of Shaka, Zulu King |
| 1833 | Abolition of slavery in British-controlled territories |
| 1836 | **Boers** undertake Great **Trek** to the interior |
| 1867 | Diamonds discovered |
| 1880–81 | First Boer War confirms Boer independence |
| 1886 | Gold discovered in Transvaal |
| 1899–1902 | Second Boer War defeats Boer republics |
| 1910 | Formation of Union of South Africa |
| 1912 | South African Native National Congress established |
| 1913 | Native Land Act limits ownership of land by blacks Nationalist Party founded |
| 1914–18 | World War I |
| 1918 | Birth of Nelson Mandela; *Broederbond* founded |
| 1920 | African miners' strike |
| 1921 | South African **Communist** party founded |
| 1922 | White miners' strike |
| 1924 | **Afrikaans** recognized as an official language |
| 1936 | Black voting rights in the Cape colony limited |
| 1939–45 | World War II |
| 1944 | ANC Youth League founded |
| 1948 | Nationalist Party government elected |
| 1950 | Suppression of Communism Act passed |
| 1952 | ANC launches Defiance Campaign |
| 1955 | ANC adopts Freedom Charter |
| 1956 | Mandela charged with treason |
| 1959 | Chief Luthuli calls for foreign **boycott** of trade with South Africa Bantu Self-Government Act passed |
| 1960 | ANC banned; police kill 69 demonstrators at Sharpeville |
| 1961 | South Africa leaves the **Commonwealth** and becomes a republic |
| 1964 | Mandela sentenced to life imprisonment South Africa banned from Olympics |
| 1966 | Prime Minister Hendrik Verwoerd is **assassinated** |
| 1976 | Soweto uprising |
| 1977 | **UN** Security Council bans arms sales to South Africa |
| 1984 | Desmond Tutu awarded Nobel Peace Prize |
| 1985 | South African government ends ban on mixed marriages |
| 1988 | Mandela's 70th birthday concert at Wembley, England |
| 1990 | Mandela released |
| 1991 | **Apartheid** laws abolished |
| 1994 | Mandela inaugurated as president of South Africa on May 10 |
| 1995 | Truth and **Reconciliation** Commission established South Africa wins Rugby World Cup |
| 1999 | Thabo Mbeki succeeds Mandela as president |

# Glossary

**activist**  someone actively involved in supporting a cause, especially in politics

**Afrikaans**  form of Dutch spoken by Afrikaners

**Afrikaner**  white Boer native speaker of Afrikaans

**apartheid**  political program to separate races

**assassinate**  to murder, especially for a political purpose

**bantustan**  area set aside for African self-government

**Boer**  in Dutch, literally means "farmer"; a white of Afrikaner descent

**boycott**  to refuse to have anything to do with a person or institution, or to refuse to buy their goods

**capital offense**  crime punishable by death

**colored**  term used in South Africa to describe those born of mixed marriages between blacks and whites

**Commonwealth**  organization of former British colonies set up to help each other through trade, aid, and training

**communist**  supporter of Communist party, which in South Africa supported violent revolution to achieve government control of all farms and businesses, and the abolition of all other political parties

**compromise**  to reach an agreement by giving up part of one's demands

**comrade**  fellow member of a political group

**constitution**  basic framework of rules about how a country is to be governed

**General Assembly**  United Nations body in which every country has an equal vote

**guerrilla**  someone who fights in a small group using hit-and-run methods

**Huguenot**  French Protestant; hundreds of thousands fled France when toleration of Protestantism ended in 1685

**invest**  to put money into a business

**kraal**  South African village of huts surrounded by a fence

**migrant**  person who leaves home in search of work or a better way of life

**militant**  aggressive, willing to risk confrontation

**oppression**  harsh rule to crush opposition

**Organization of African Unity**  organization founded in 1963 to promote cooperation among African states, to end colonial rule in Africa, and to raise African living standards. South Africa joined in 1994.

**reconciliation**  overcoming past disagreements to become friends

**representative**  someone who speaks on behalf of another person or group

**sabotage**  deliberate destruction, usually for a political purpose

**sanction**  form of punishment, such as refusal to trade

**terrorism**  acts of violence committed for political reasons

**trek**  Afrikaans word meaning "journey"

**United Nations (UN)**  organization founded in 1945 to promote international cooperation; almost every country in the world belongs

# More Books to Read

Bradley, Catherine. *The End of Apartheid.* Austin, Tex.: Raintree Steck-Vaughn Publishers, 1995.

Meisel, Jacqueline D. *South Africa at the Crossroads.* Brookfield, Conn.: Milbrook Press, Inc., 1994.

Pratt, Paula B. *The End of Apartheid in South Africa.* San Diego, Calif.: Lucent Books, 1995.

# Index